presents

ULTIMATE SURVIVOR

WHICH AUSSIE ANIMAL WILL TRIUMPH AS AUSTRALIA'S GREATEST SURVIVOR?

IT'S QUITE OBVIOUS THAT I'M AUSTRALIA'S TOUGHEST SURVIVOR. HAVE YOU SEEN MY ARMS, BY THE WAY?
YOU COULDN'T HANDLE THE KIND OF PRESSURE I'M UNDER, ROO-BOY.
HA! NO WAY YOU'D SSSSURVIVE IN THE BIG SSSSMOKE, BUDDY.
I'D LIKE TO SEE YOU SURVIVE MINUS 25 DEGREES WITH FIVE HUNGRY CHICKS TO FEED. YOU WOULDN'T LAST A MINUTE!
TRY GOING WITHOUT A DRINK FOR A COUPLE OF DAYS, TOUGH GUY.
...OR LIVING NEXT DOOR TO HUMANS. WHAT A MESS!
LET THE SHOWDOWN BEGIN!

ULTIMATE SURVIVOR

For some of nature's Ultimate Survivors, like our Survivors of Extinction (see page 24) that have bounced back from the edge of oblivion, survival has been mostly a matter of good luck. They've hung onto life, hidden away in isolated pockets, avoiding the threats that have pushed their species close to extinction. Generally, however, the sure way to be a survivor in nature is to be good – really good – at the things that give you an edge.

Take the Wollemi pine, for example (see page 19). A protective waxy coating that covers its growing buds during the cold months is thought to have helped this hardy species survive many ice ages. Or what about the deep-sea coffinfish, which, as well as having all those other specialist features of deep-sea creatures, carries its own fishing rod tipped with a fluffy bait on top of its head to attract prey in a world where there's very little food?

Then there's the crucifix frog that endures hot, dry conditions by living underground, wrapping itself in a protective cocoon, and taking advantage of the first drops of rain to breed like crazy – before disappearing to its secret hideaway again. And you've got to be impressed by the southern elephant seal, which can dive and survive deeper under the ocean than any other seal on the planet– and most other mammals, as a matter of fact – by developing a range of amazing body adaptations.

But our pick for the Ultimate Survivor Grand Champion (see page 28) has created habits and tactics to ensure it can endure almost anything the natural world throws its way. This amazing little creature can withstand extreme heat, high pressure, very low temperatures and pretty much everything else that this world (and beyond) can throw at it. Read on to meet all the incredible contenders...

Survivors of EXTREME COLD

Despite its vast deserts, Australia does have some cold – even alpine – places, both on the mainland and in Tasmania. You'll find plenty of species there specially adapted to surviving very cold weather. Australia also has some of the coolest places on Earth in some of its offshore territories, notably in Antarctica, where you'll also find some of the world's best survivors of cold.

The CONTENDERS

EMPEROR PENGUIN

AKA *Aptenodytes forsteri*

SIZE About 1.2m tall **SURVIVAL TACTIC** Adults with chicks and eggs huddle together to stay warm

Adult emperor penguins have multiple layers of feathers to keep out freezing blizzards in Antarctica, where they breed. They also have lots of body fat to provide them with energy and insulation. Another adaptation is they can 'recycle' their own body heat. This is done by blood flowing away from the heart in arteries, passing close to veins travelling in the other direction. This means that blood is pre-cooled as it heads towards the penguin's feet, wings and bill, but warmed on its way back to the heart.

HUDDLE CLOSE, KIDS. WHEN MUMMY GETS COLD SHE GETS CRANKY.

SURVIVAL KIT

Special fats in the emperor penguin's feet stop them from freezing.

I STILL WOULDN'T SAY NO TO A PAIR OF WARM FLIPPER SLIPPERS, THOUGH.

SURVIVOR SCORE

6/10

CORROBOREE FROGS

AKA *Pseudophryne spp.*

SIZE 3cm **SURVIVAL TACTIC** Adults enter a type of winter hibernation known as torpor

There are two species of corroboree frog. Both are found in a very small area around Kosciusko National Park and the Snowy Mountains. And sadly, despite their ultimate survival tactics, both are critically endangered due to a fungal disease and other problems caused by humans. They have the same sort of life cycle as most other frogs: tadpoles hatch from eggs and live in water until they change into adults, when they live on land. In corroboree frogs, however, the eggs develop at first but stop growing for a while and enter what's known as a 'diapause'. They start developing again and then hatch after rainfall or snow melt late in winter floods their nest.

LOVE YOUR PYJAMAS!

SURVIVOR SCORE 7/10

THANKS! I WAS PLANNING TO SPEND A LOT OF TIME IN BED THIS YEAR.

SURVIVAL KIT

By accumulating poisons in their skin from the ants they eat, corroboree frogs are protected from predators.

COD ICEFISHES

AKA *Notothenia spp.*

SIZE There are several species, ranging in size from 30–90cm long
SURVIVAL TACTIC Antifreeze in the blood

These are not really cods but they're certainly icefishes, specially adapted to surviving in the bitterly cold waters of the Southern Ocean around Antarctica. They have a special protein in their blood that acts like an antifreeze to stop the blood from freezing in the icy conditions.

I'M ODD. BUT NOT A COD. BUT DEFINITELY COLD.

SURVIVOR SCORE 8/10

BOGONG MOTH

AKA *Agrotis infusa*

SIZE 2.5–5cm **SURVIVAL TACTIC** Staying dormant over the summer

Millions of adult bogong moths spend summer in a dormant state, living off fat reserves, in rock crevices in the Australian Alps. But as winter approaches they all take off in a mass migration heading for breeding grounds in Queensland and NSW. In summer, they fly back the other way to return to the mountains. They've been doing the same thing and following the same migration routes for thousands of years.

SO...YOU GUYS GOT PLANS FOR LUNCH?

SURVIVOR SCORE

7/10

MOUNTAIN PYGMY POSSUM

AKA *Burramys parvus*

SIZE About 10cm long
SURVIVAL TACTIC Hibernating during winter

The mountain pygmy possum is the only Australian mammal that lives permanently in an alpine region. It can do this because it fattens itself up for a winter hibernation by gorging in summer on Bogong moths. Then in winter it curls up in a ball under an insulating layer of snow and hibernates through the coldest months of the year.

SURVIVAL STORY

The mountain pygmy possum was thought to be extinct before it was rediscovered in the 1960s.

LEOPARD SEAL

AKA *Hydrurga leptonyx*

SIZE Females, which are larger than males, can weigh up to 500kg
SURVIVAL TACTIC Being big with lots of body fat

A thick layer of fat known as blubber helps to keep elephant seals warm in the freezing waters of Antarctica, where they hunt for penguins. Being a large size also helps mammals, such as these seals, stay warmer in cold conditions because they have more muscle to generate heat and less body area to lose it from. These predatory seals can survive in sub-zero sea temperatures.

ULTIMATE FACT!
The only predators of leopard seals are killer whales.

SURVIVOR SCORE
9/10

★ TOURNAMENT ROUND ★

Survivors of DESERTS

Much of Australia is hot and dry. In fact, after Antarctica, Australia is the driest continent in the world. About a third of the Australian mainland receives so little rain that it could be classified as desert and three-quarters is so dry that it is classified as arid or semi-arid. And yet, there are plenty of animal species surviving in these places – you just might need to look hard for them.

SURVIVOR SCORE
5/10

The CONTENDERS

SURVIVAL KIT

The spinifex hopping mouse has the most efficient kidneys of any mammal in the world.

THORNY DEVIL

AKA *Moloch horridus*

SIZE 20cm long **SURVIVAL TACTIC** Water-catching skin

The thorny devil comes out by day to feed on small insects. Its body colouration makes it hard for its main predators, birds of prey, to see it against desert sands. The spikes all over its body are for defence and also a clever to catch dew drops, which the devil collects each morning by rubbing up against spinifex. Through a process known as capillary action, the tiny droplets of water run down the grooves between the spikes and straight into the devil's mouth.

ANYONE KNOW WHERE A THIRSTY DEVIL CAN GET A DRINK AROUND HERE?

SURVIVOR SCORE
6/10

NOPE. BUT I KNOW A GREAT LITTLE UNDERGROUND PLACE THAT DOES TASTY SNACKS.

SPINIFEX HOPPING MOUSE

AKA *Notomys alexis*

SIZE 8cm long **SURVIVAL TACTIC** Near-solid urine

Like many desert mammals, this little native Australian rodent avoids the daytime heat and only comes out at night to forage for food. It has ultra-efficient kidneys that remove every last drop of water from its urine, making it almost solid. Because of this, the spinifex hopping mouse can survive for long periods without drinking water.

SOUTHERN MARSUPIAL MOLE

AKA *Notoryctes typhlops*

SIZE 12cm long **SURVIVAL TACTIC** Living almost exclusively underground

This endangered desert dweller is a superb burrower, that 'swims' rather than digs through sand. It leads with a calloused nose and forehead, which is followed through by its spade-shaped feet and well-developed shoulders. Because marsupial moles need very little oxygen they can survive by breathing in air trapped between sand grains.

SURVIVOR SCORE 8/10

BILBY

AKA *Macrotis lagotis*

SIZE Males up to 55cm long, females up to 39cm, both with a 20-29cm long tail
SURVIVAL TACTIC Having oversized, furless ears

Bilbies use their strong front limbs to dig deep, corkscrew-shaped, underground burrows, where they shelter from the desert sun. Their huge, near-naked ears help release body heat, but also gives bilbies very good hearing to find their insect prey at night.

SURVIVAL KIT

While bilbies have outstanding senses of smell and hearing, they have extremely poor eyesight.

SURVIVOR SCORE 6/10

CRUCIFIX FROG

AKA *Notaden bennettii*

SIZE 6.5 cm long **SURVIVAL TACTIC** Living underground inside a protective cocoon

This burrowing, arid-zone frog can live in a type of suspended animation up to 3m underground for years at a time, waiting for rain. At the first few drops it digs its way to the surface to feed and breed like crazy before heading back underground to wait for the next shower. It keeps moist while underground by secreting a protective cocoon around itself.

SURVIVAL KIT

The bright colours of the crucifix frog are a warning sign to predators that it's too poisonous to eat.

CAMEL

AKA *Camelus dromedarius*

SIZE Up to 2m tall
SURVIVAL TACTIC Almost every aspect of a camel's physiology is adapted to living in the desert

Camels are not native to Australia. They were brought here by British settlers in the 1800s, mainly for use as outback transport. But they are so superbly adapted to the desert environment that their numbers grew and grew. Now, Central Australia has one of the world's largest populations of dromedary camels – about one million.

SURVIVAL SKILL

Camels respond to the desert heat by reducing their urine production and sweating economically.

RED KANGAROO

AKA *Macropus rufus*

SIZE Males are bigger, growing to more than 1.8 m tall
SURVIVAL TACTIC Remaining inactive during the hottest part of the day

Using strong hind legs, the red kangaroo can cover almost 8m in a single leap and bound across desert sands at speeds of almost 60km per hour. It's a great way to travel to distant food patches in arid areas. One of their many adaptations to desert survival is on their forearms: there they have a dense network of blood vessels near the skin's surface. Red kangaroos lick this area and through a process called evaporative cooling, heat from inside the body is released and blows away in the desert wind.

ULTIMATE FACT!
Red kangaroos are the largest of Australia's marsupials.

WHO YOU CALLING BEEFCAKE? YOU WANNA TAKE THIS OUTSIDE, JOEY?

★ TOURNAMENT ROUND ★

Survivors of THE DEEP

Just like it is the world over, the deep sea off Australia is our least explored habitat. What we do know is that there's a lack of light and food down there and it's cold. Plus, the immense weight of the ocean pressing down means it's a place where animals are exposed to great pressure. Being on the bottom of the deep sea can be like having a plane sitting on top of you! To visit there, an animal has to have some very special adaptations. And the creatures that live there need even more extreme survival tactics.

The CONTENDERS

BLOBFISH
AKA *Pychrolutes marcidus*

SIZE 30cm **SURVIVAL TACTIC** Lacking a skeleton

The blobfish lives about 1000m down in waters off Australia and New Zealand. At that depth the surrounding pressure is 120 times what it is on the surface and would crush a body with bones. And so the blobfish has no bones. Its soft body mass is instead supported by the surrounding pressure. In its own deep-sea environment, the blobfish would look a lot more like a normal fish, not the blobby mess it collapses into when it's been brought up to the surface by deep-sea trawlers!

SURVIVAL SKILL
The blobfish literally floats in the water just above the ocean bottom, waiting to make a meal out of passing crustaceans or molluscs.

SURVIVOR SCORE 6/10

DON'T CALL ME BLOBBY. I'M UNDER A LOT OF PRESSURE.

Photograph: Kerryn Parkins @ The Australian Museum.

COFFINFISH
AKA *Chaunacidae*

SIZE 20-30cm
SURVIVAL TACTIC Carrying its own fishing rod

The mysterious little deep-sea coffinfishes have blue eyes and red feet, and belong to the anglerfish group. They live up to 2km deep underwater off Australia and attract unsuspecting prey using a fishing lure on the top of their heads.

SURVIVAL SKILL
When threatened, coffinfishes often inflate themselves to look more menacing.

SURVIVOR SCORE 7/10

LIFE'S TOUGH AT THE BOTTOM, RIGHT BLOBBY?

DOES MY BREATH SMELL FISHY?

SOUTHERN ELEPHANT SEAL

AKA *Mirounga leonina*

SIZE Males, which are much bigger than females, can reach a length of 4m and a weight of 3 tonnes **SURVIVAL TACTIC** Special blood

Elephant seals have been recorded diving to 2km below the surface. No other seal can do that. A range of special adaptations to conserve and create energy in their bodies allow elephant seals to make these massive dives. Firstly, there's that body shape, which underwater looks like a torpedo and means they can glide through the water effortlessly. Then there's a range of special features about their blood that mean they can take a breath and make the oxygen last for hours.

SURVIVOR SCORE
9/10

IT IS A BIT WHIFFY. I'D SEA KELP IF I WERE YOU.

ZOMBIE WORMS
AKA *Osedax spp.*

SIZE 2-7cm
SURVIVAL TACTIC Scavenging inside bones

These deep-sea worms are often found in the decaying remains of whales on the ocean floor. They burrow deep into the bones of these animal corpses to reach the nutritious substance within and feed on that. But they have no functioning mouth, stomach or anus, and so they use bacteria living inside them to digest these grisly bits for them.

SURVIVOR SCORE 7/10

SEA PIGS
AKA *Elpidiidae*

SURVIVOR SCORE 6/10

SIZE Up to 15cm long **SURVIVAL TACTIC** Living on animal tissue that rains from above

There aren't, of course, any pigs, which are mammals, living in the deep ocean. Sea pigs are actually sea cucumbers – a group of animals related to sea urchins and starfish. They're plump little creatures with as many as seven pairs of 'legs' that they use to trundle across the seafloor, grazing down as far down as 6km. Sea pigs have mouths ringed by feeding tentacles that they use to vacuum up bits of debris from the sea floor, such as tiny pieces of tissue that float down from rotting whale carcasses above.

ORANGE ROUGHY
AKA *Hoplostethus atlanticus*

SIZE About 50cm long and 7kg **SURVIVAL TACTIC** Being orange

Scientists used to call these deep-sea fish slimeheads. The common name was changed when people began catching them to eat and the name slimehead didn't make it sound appealing. It's now known as the orange roughy and like that name suggests it's coloured orange. This is a predatory fish, and you'd think that colour would make it stand out to prey it's trying to catch. But at the depths where it lives – 700 to 1400m below the ocean's surface off southern Australia – there's either no light or very little red light, so being orange makes it seem invisible.

SURVIVOR SCORE 6/10

JUST BEFORE I DIVE AGAIN... DO YOU HAVE ANY GOOD WHALE SONG RECOMMENDATIONS?

CUVIER'S BEAKED WHALE

AKA *Ziphius cavirostris*

SIZE 7m long, 3 tonnes in weight
SURVIVAL TACTIC Having flipper pockets and collapsible lungs

This whale has been recorded diving to almost 3km deep and staying underwater for more than three hours at a time. That's deeper and longer than any other whale species. Whales, of course, breath air so exactly how they can spend so much time underwater so deep and for so long is yet to be understood. They do, however, have one particular amazing adaptation we know of that helps them reach so deeply. They have pocket-like folds on the sides of their bodies, where they can tuck away their flippers to make them more streamlined so they can glide through the water. It's also thought that they may also be able to collapse their rib cage and lungs to cope with the extreme pressure of the deep sea.

NOT REALLY... I MUCH PREFER LISTENING TO PODCASTS WHILST DIVING.

SURVIVOR SCORE
8/10

HOW NOT TO SURVIVE

One of the few times we see Cuvier's beaked whales is when they accidentally strand themselves on beaches along the coast of Australia and New Zealand.

★ TOURNAMENT ROUND ★

Survivors of TIME

Australia's animals and plants have been evolving in isolation – separated from much of the rest of the world – for many millions of years. It's why as much as 80 per cent of our fauna is unique and doesn't occur anywhere else in the world. Being isolated from the rest of the world for so long has helped us retain a high proportion of 'living fossils' – species that haven't changed, in some cases, since the age of dinosaurs. These are a few of those Ultimate Survivors of Time.

ULTIMATE FACT!
Even the egg of the giant panda snail is huge – about the size of a small bird's egg.

The CONTENDERS

VELVET WORM
AKA *Euperipatoides rowelli*

SIZE 3-10cm **SPECIES AGE** Hundreds of millions of years
SURVIVAL TACTIC Having sticky prey-catching slime

The unusual way this velvet worm, found in south-east Australia's temperate forests, catches prey, could be a secret to the species' lengthy survival. It hides in rotting logs and leaf litter and subdues small invertebrates, such as termites and centipedes, by covering them with a net of sticky slime excreted from glands on its head. Then it eats into its prey's skin and sucks out the nutritious fluids.

SURVIVOR SCORE 8/10

GIANT PANDA SNAIL
AKA *Hedleyella faconeri*

SURVIVOR SCORE 6/10

SIZE 9cm-high shell **SPECIES AGE**: 85 million years
SURVIVAL TACTIC Only coming out when it rains

Being about the size of a tennis ball, the giant panda snail is Australia's largest land snail. It's thought to have been living, unchanged, in the same place since it evolved when Australia was still attached to Antarctica and India. That's when Australia was covered in warm moist and forests and today that's still where you'll find it, in southern Queensland and northern NSW.

SURVIVAL SKILL
Cyanobacteria were the first known organisms on Earth to photosynthesis and produce oxygen – they're like the earliest plants.

SURVIVOR SCORE
8/10

ULTIMATE FACT!
It's thought that a Queensland lungfish can live for up to 100 years.

AUSTRALIAN LUNGFISH
AKA *Neoceratodus forsteri*

SIZE Up to 150cm long **SPECIES AGE** 400 million years
SURVIVAL TACTIC Breathing air when necessary

If you look back far enough, you'll see that all life on Earth started out in the ocean. Species such as the Australian lungfish provide a clue about how that transition might have happened: although they live mostly aquatic lives they can also survive amazingly well out of water for a while. This species has a fully functional lung, to breathe air directly, as well as the gills of a fish, to absorb oxygen from water. This means it can survive in drying up water holes during long periods of drought.

STROMATOLITES
AKA *Cyanobacteria*

SIZE Microscopic **SPECIES AGE** Up to 3.5 billion years
SURVIVAL TACTIC Increasing oxygen levels in the air

Until 1961 stromatolites were only known from fossils. But we now know living colonies remain in a few isolated sites in WA and Tasmania. Stromatolites are layered rock-like structures trapped and built up over thousands of years by colonies of microscopic organisms called cyanobacteria. These harness energy from sunlight and produce oxygen in the process. Very early on in the history of life they were very abundant on our planet.

SURVIVOR SCORE
7/10

★ TOURNAMENT ROUND ★

ANY OF YOU OLD FELLAS SEEN MY DISTANT RELATIVE, THE ECHIDNA, ROUND HERE?

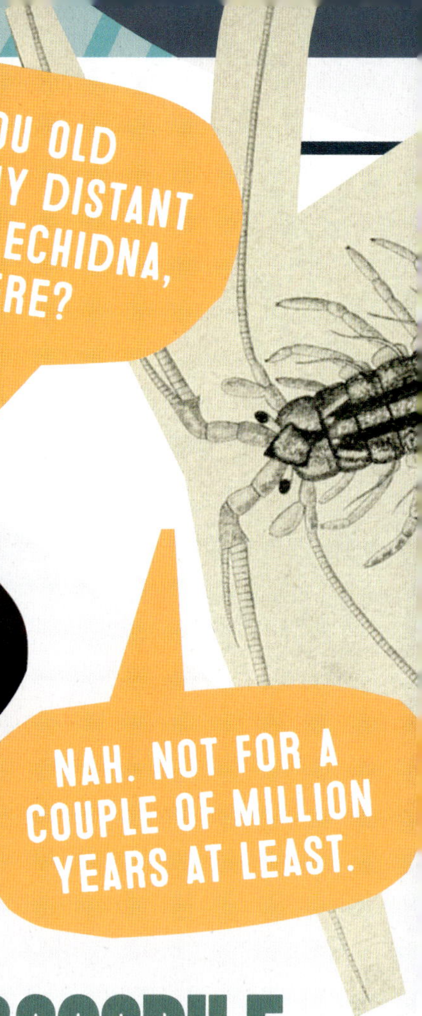

NAH. NOT FOR A COUPLE OF MILLION YEARS AT LEAST.

ULTIMATE FACT!
When British scientists in the 18th Century first saw a platypus skin sent from Australia, they thought it was a hoax, created by stitching different together different parts of other animals.

SURVIVOR SCORE 7/10

PLATYPUS

AKA *Ornithorhynchus anatinus*

SIZE Reach lengths of 40-60cm (females are smaller) **SPECIES AGE** The oldest platypus fossils come from 61-million-year-old rocks in South America. **SURVIVAL TACTIC** Special antibacterial proteins in the milk of mother platypuses protect their babies

The platypus is grouped with echidnas into a separate group of mammals called monotremes. Like reptiles they lay eggs, but like other mammals they nurture their young with milk, which suggests they are like a missing link between the two groups.

SALTWATER CROCODILE

AKA *Crocodylus porosis*

SIZE Males grow to 6m and weigh up to 1000kg **SPECIES AGE** 55 million years **SURVIVAL TACTIC** Being at the top of the food chain

If this northern Australian species wasn't around when dinosaurs ruled the Earth, then species that were very similar were. It's perfectly adapted to its environment and is thought to have remained virtually unchanged for more than 50 millions of years.

SURVIVAL KIT
The saltwater crocodile is the largest living reptile species on Earth.

NOPE. I'M JUST TRYING TO KEEP A LOW PROFILE.

SURVIVOR SCORE 9/10

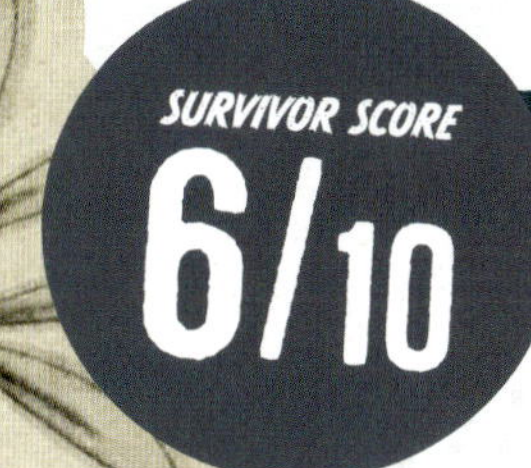

MOUNTAIN SHRIMP

AKA *Anaspididae*

SIZE: Up to 6cm long **SPECIES AGE** 220 million years **SURVIVAL TACTIC** Adapting to very tough habitat – high-country, cold-water Tasmanian streams and caves

This freshwater shrimp species lives only in Tasmania, but is related to shrimps found in South America and New Zealand. This suggests it must have evolved before Australia split away from those landmasses about 180 million years ago. Fossils found in lake sediments in NSW are almost identical to this Tasmanian species and are 220 million years old.

ULTIMATE FACT! Dinosaurs would have munched on the branches of the Wollemi pine.

SURVIVOR SCORE 9/10

WOLLEMI PINE

AKA *Wollemi nobilia*

SIZE Can grow to 30m high
SPECIES AGE 200 million years
SURVIVAL TACTIC A protective waxy coating that covers growing buds during cold months, is thought to have helped the Wollemi pine survive many ice ages

This tree, which was discovered in 1994 in Wollemi National Park west of Sydney, NSW, is known as "the botanical find of the 20th Century". There are fewer than 100 adult trees known to survive in the wild. Their exact whereabouts is kept secret to protect them.

SHORT-BEAKED ECHIDNA

AKA *Tachyglossus aculeatus*

SIZE 40–50cm long, up to 6kg
SPECIES AGE More than 23 million years
SURVIVAL TACTIC Adapting to a wide range of habitats, from alpine areas to the edges of deserts

This species of ant-eating, egg-laying mammal is only found in Australia, although it has close relatives in Papua New Guinea. It has one of the widest distributions across Australia of any native mammal. So far, the oldest-known fossil echidna has been dated to 17 million years ago and was found in a cave in eastern Australia, but the species is thought to be older.

Survivors of URBAN SPRAWL

Some animal species cope better than others with spreading cities. Natural habitat provides animals with places to sleep and shelter, and food to eat. And most species find the habitat destruction that comes with urban sprawl is impossible to cope with, so they move away or their numbers dwindle. Sadly, some even become extinct. But for a few species – those that aren't so fussy about what they eat or where they sleep – urban sprawl and the arrival of people has boosted their survival.

The CONTENDERS

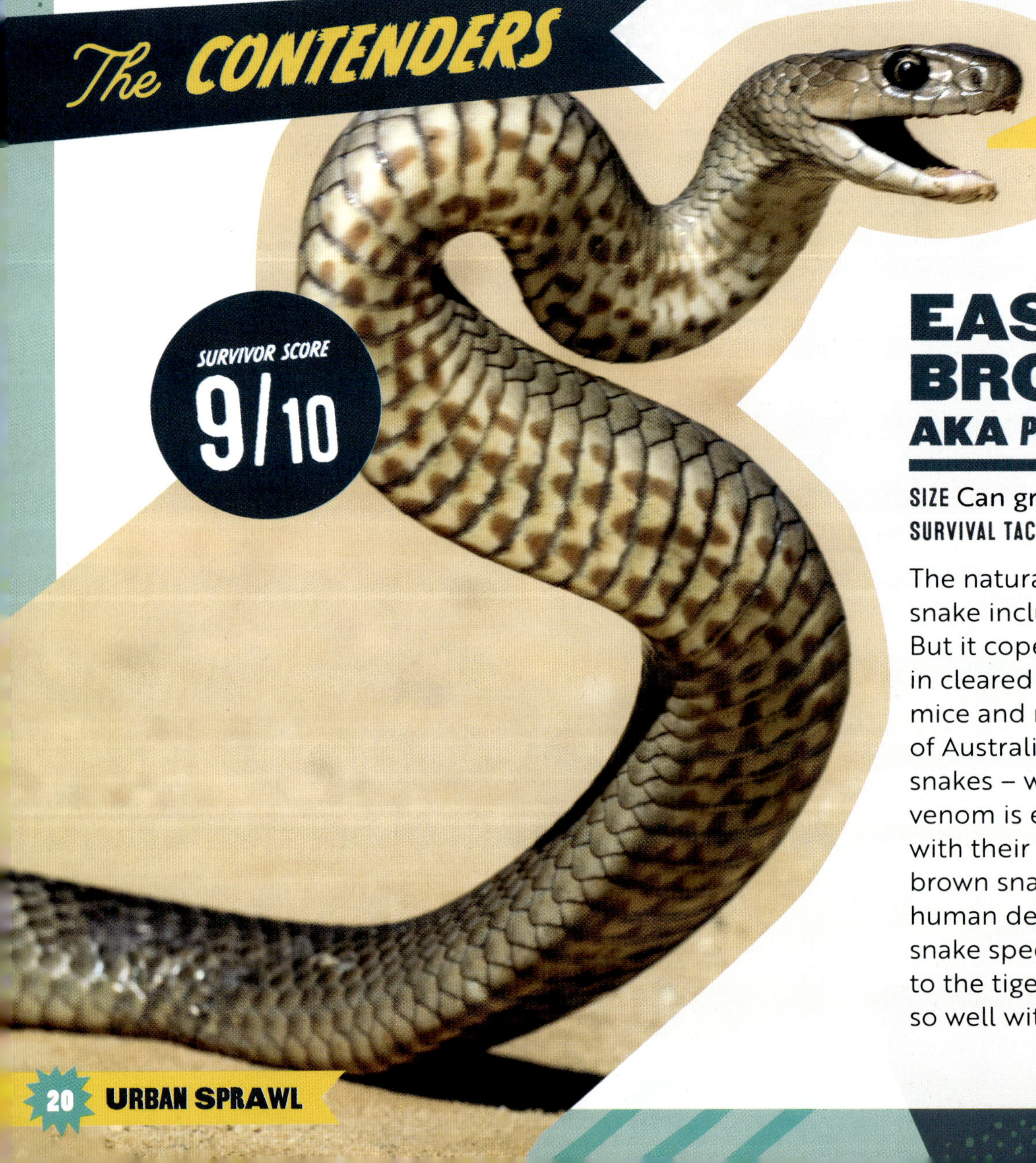

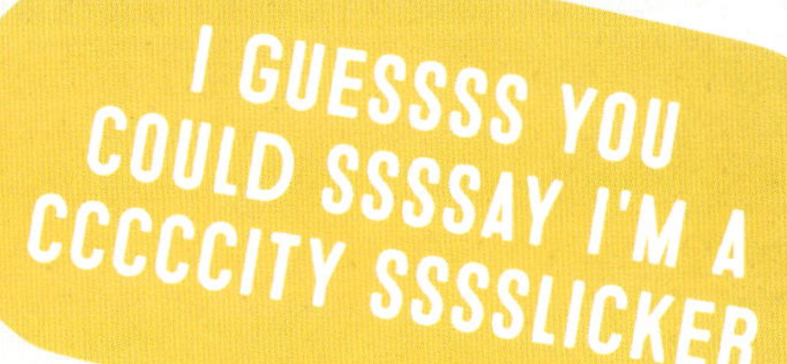

SURVIVOR SCORE
9/10

EASTERN BROWN SNAKE

AKA *Pseudonaja textilis*

SIZE Can grow to a length of 2.4m
SURVIVAL TACTIC Eating introduced species

The natural habitat of the eastern brown snake includes woodlands and grasslands. But it copes well with human activity, thrives in cleared areas and loves to eat introduced mice and rats. Because of that it's now one of Australia's most commonly encountered snakes – which is unfortunate because its venom is extremely potent. This, coupled with their wide distribution, now sees brown snakes being responsible for more human deaths in Australia than any other snake species. That title used to belong to the tiger snake, which hasn't coped so well with urban sprawl.

THE CITY'S OK BUT I'M STILL A COUNTRY BOY AT HEART. LOVE MY GRAINS.

GALAH

AKA *Eolophus roseicapilla*

SIZE Up to 35cm **SURVIVAL TACTIC** Adapting to human crops

The spread of agriculture across Australia has seen the numbers of this pink-and- grey parrot boom since Europeans first arrived here 234 years ago. They are seed-eaters and have adapted well to many grain crops grown by humans, such as wheat and barley. The species used to be restricted to much of the continent's inland areas, but it's now found throughout Australia, including coastal areas. Galahs are now even in Tasmania, for example, and were never there naturally.

SURVIVOR SCORE
6/10

WE LOVE THE CITY AND IT'S DIVERSE SELECTION OF WATERING HOLES. AND REAL ESTATE.

SURVIVOR SCORE
7/10

RAINBOW LORIKEET

AKA *Trichoglossus haematodus*

SIZE Up to 30cm long
SURVIVAL TACTIC Aggressive behaviour

This parrot was the 'most sighted bird' in Australia in 2020. That's probably partly to do with the fact that they're loud and colourful, which makes them hard to miss. But there's also a lot of them in our cities, and they're now found way beyond where they originally occurred in eastern and northern Australia. These days they're also found much further west, even as far as Perth, thousands of kilometres outside of their natural range. Their aggression there has stopped some local bird species from nesting.

ULTIMATE FACT!
Rainbow lorikeets have been seen taking over nesting hollows of local species in Perth, dragging their nestlings out and dropping them on the ground.

SURVIVAL SKILL
Peregrine falcons are the fastest animals in the world, swooping on prey at speeds of up to 320km per hour.

WHAT'S THAT RACKET?

SURVIVOR SCORE 6/10

PEREGRINE FALCON

AKA *Falco peregrinus*

SIZE 35-55cm
SURVIVAL TACTIC Building nests on skyscrapers

Peregrine falcons live all over the world and have adapted well to life in many big cities, including those in Australia. They particularly like tall buildings because, being birds of prey, these give them a high vantage point from where they can watch for prey. They will even make their nests on the window ledges of skyscrapers. These falcons also like to eat introduced rats and mice and you'll sometimes see peregrine falcons soaring above our cities looking for prey. In this way they perform a kind of pest-control role.

SORRY! BEEN CHIPPING AWAY AT THIS BANJO THING. FAT FINGERS.

EASTERN BANJO FROG

AKA *Limnodynastes dumerilii*

SIZE 7.5cm long
SURVIVAL TACTIC Being highly adaptable

Frogs often don't survive well in urban areas, but the banjo frog has. There are five subspecies surviving in cities and suburbs right across eastern Australia, including Tasmania. They like to live near water, so backyard ponds and waterways near city parks suit them well.

SURVIVOR SCORE 6/10

SO... DID SOMEONE SAY CHIP?

SILVER GULL

AKA *Chroicocephalus novaehollandiae*

SIZE Up to 45cm **SURVIVAL TACTIC** Aggressive scavenging

Yes, this is that bird that flocks around us at the beach begging for our hot chips. There weren't always so many silver gulls in Australia. But they do very well surviving in our cities, living off our food scraps and their numbers have exploded since the middle of last century. They breed alongside other seabirds at colonies on islands off Australia's coasts. But there are now so many silver gulls at these sites that they force out other birds, like terns.

SURVIVOR SCORE 7/10

BRUSHTAIL POSSUM

AKA *Trichosurus vulpecula*

SIZE Up to 55cm long, plus a tail of 25-40cm; up to 4.5kg in weight.
SURVIVAL TACTIC Eating a range of foods.

This species occurs in a wide range of natural habitats, from rainforest and arid zone woodlands to eucalypt forests. But it's a highly adaptable mammal and survives well in disturbed landscapes in and around Australia's cities and towns, where it's found in parks and backyards with a lot of trees. Brushtail possums have even been known to move into and live in the roofs of people's homes. Brushtails were introduced to New Zealand in the mid-1800s to support a fur industry and adjusted so well to life there that their population grew enormously, and the species spread right across the country.

SURVIVE & THRIVE

Brushtail possum numbers have grown so much in New Zealand since it was introduced there that it's now become widely hated as one of New Zealand's worst feral pests.

★ TOURNAMENT ROUND ★

Survivors of EXTINCTION

HEY SWAMPY!

Extinction is a natural part of life on Earth. But Australia is now facing an extinction crisis and losing species at an unnatural rate – faster than ever before. And that's due to us. Through things like clearing the forests, pollution and climate change, our actions are forcing many animal species to the brink of existence. But occasionally a species we thought we'd lost forever is found. Here are a lucky few survivors of extinction.

The CONTENDERS

WESTERN SWAMP TORTOISE

AKA *Pseudemydura umbrina*

SIZE Up to 15.5cm **SURVIVAL TACTIC** Clinging to survival in a small area of natural habitat where foxes haven't yet reached

This is Australia's rarest reptile. It was thought to have been extinct for more than 100 years, when it was rediscovered in 1953. Its main threats have been habitat destruction and predation by introduced predators, like foxes and feral pigs. There are now still only two wild populations of this reptile, both near Perth. Another two populations have been established and captive breeding is building the species' numbers. It is, however, still critically endangered.

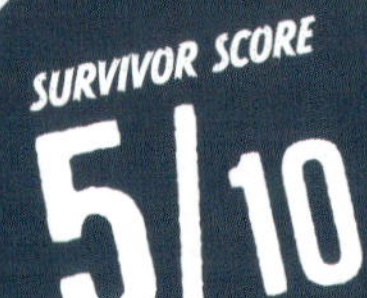

NIGHT PARROT

AKA *Pezoporus occidentalis*

SURVIVOR SCORE 5/10

SIZE Up to 25cm
SURVIVAL TACTIC Hiding out in small, undisturbed areas

This very rare species of parrot lives on the ground, is active at night, and is threatened by feral cats. During the 1800s it been reported from arid and semi-arid areas in all mainland states. But from the early 1900s there were no confirmed records of it for almost 80 years and it was presumed to be extinct. Then it was rediscovered in 2013 in western Queensland. Since then, at least two tiny populations have also been found in Western Australia. The species is now classified as endangered.

I WASN'T SURE IF I'D SEE YOU AGAIN. IT'S GREAT TO HAVE YOU BACK!

LORD HOWE ISLAND STICK INSECT

AKA *Dryococelus australis*

SIZE 20cm **SURVIVAL TACTIC** Living in a remote area away from its main threat

Also known as a tree lobster, this very large insect was thought to have been hunted to extinction last century by black rats, which had been introduced to its Lord Howe Island home. Then in 2001 climbers discovered a small number clinging to life on a tiny volcanic outcrop called Balls Pyramid, located in treacherous ocean waters about 20km off Lord Howe. Two breeding pairs of the insect were recovered in 2003 and have since been used to build up numbers of the species. This unusual stick insect is now classified as critically endangered.

SURVIVOR SCORE
7/10

ULTIMATE HIDEOUT

Balls Pyramid is so hard to get onto and off that it took two years for rangers to plan the rescue mission to recover some of the surviving Lord Howe Island stick insects.

EASTERN BARRED BANDICOOT

AKA *Perameles gunnii*

SIZE 40cm long (including their tail); average weight: 800g
SURVIVAL TACTICS Captive breeding, fox eradication

This marsupial, which is about the size of a rabbit, used to be common across Victoria. But predation by feral foxes and habitat destruction caused its numbers to plummet and it was declared extinct in the wild in that state. Then bandicoots that had been bred at a zoo were introduced onto two islands in Victoria's Westernport Bay. Because feral predators had been removed from the islands, those bandicoots were safe and their numbers grew. By 2021 there were more than 1500 bandicoots in those populations. Victoria's official conservation status for the species was then changed from 'extinct in the wild' to 'endangered'.

SURVIVOR SCORE
6/10

CREST-TAILED MULGARA

AKA *Dasycercus cristicauda*

SIZE Up to 30cm long (including the tail): weight of 190g **SURVIVAL TACTICS** Staying in very remote areas

No one had seen this little marsupial carnivore in New South Wales for more than a century and it was classified as extinct in the state – another victim of introduced feral animals! Then, in 2017, the crest-tailed mulgara was rediscovered in arid country in the state's far north-west. The species is now off NSW's extinction list but is still classified as Near Threatened.

ME NEITHER. SUCH PESTS!

CAN'T LIVE WITH THEM! THEY SHOULD MAKE THEM ALL WEAR BELLS.

NUMBAT

AKA *Myrmecobius fasciatus*

SIZE About 35cm long, including its tail; weighs less than 700g. **SURVIVAL TACTICS** Feral fox and cat eradication programs

Extinction came very close twice in the late 20th Century for the numbat. This tiny, striped marsupial used to live right across southern Australia but by the 1980s only two natural populations survived. Both were in Western Australia. Numbats' biggest threats have been foxes and then cats. A fox eradication program in WA saw numbat numbers bounce back. Then feral cats moved in and killed so many numbats that the species almost went extinct again. A successful feral cat eradication program has now seen numbat numbers rise again.

SURVIVOR SCORE 7/10

SURVIVAL KIT
The numbat has a long sticky tongue that it uses to eat termites – more than 20,000 every day!

WATER BEAR

AKA Tardigrade

SIZE Almost microscopic **SURVIVAL TACTIC** Cryptobiosis

If any organisms on Earth deserves the title of Ultimate Survivor, it must be the tardigrades. These ultra-tiny, eight-legged creatures with plump pig-like bodies are not closely related to any other living animals and are almost indestructible. They were first discovered in 1773 and there are now more than 1300 known species. They can survive high pressure, excess salt, a complete lack of water, extremely low temperatures, high levels of UV radiation ... and pretty much anything else you can throw at them. It's even thought that they may have survived the crash of a lander on the moon in 2019. When conditions get too extreme, however, tardigrades can continue to survive by entering a kind of extreme suspended animation called cryptobiosis – sometimes for decades at a time, after which they can be revived when conditions improve.

SURVIVAL SKILL

The death-like state that a water bear enters to survive really extreme conditions is called cryptobiosis. During this, it expels almost all the water from its body, retracts its head and legs, and curls up into a desiccated ball.

I BELIEVE WE MAY HAVE MET ON THE MOON, MANY MOONS AGO.

AND SINCE THEN... I'VE BEEN WAITING IN SUSPENDED ANIMATION FOR YOU TO CALL.

GRAND

AUSTRALIA'S ULTIMATE SURVIVOR

CHAMPION

GLOSSARY

Adaptation: A change or adjustment.

Alpine: Related to the mountains or a mountainous environment.

Blubber: Thick body fat that protects against the cold.

Camouflaged: Hidden by blending in.

Crustaceans: A group of animals, mostly found in the sea, with shells and often claws – includes crabs, prawns and krill.

Cryptobiosis: A creature's ability to bring their metabolism to a complete – but reversible – standstill.

Dormant: Inactive; in a state of rest.

Feral: A domesticated animal that's been allowed to live freely in an environment it's not native to.

Hibernation: Staying in one place and being inactive over the winter months.

Immense: Very, very big.

Invertebrates: Animals without a backbone, like spiders and insects.

Living fossils: Species that haven't changed since the age of dinosaurs.

Molluscs: A group of animals with soft bodies often covered in shells. Includes snails, slugs, squids, octopuses and mussels.

Monotremes: Egg-laying mammals such as the platypus and echidna.

Nestling: A baby bird that's too young to leave the nest.

Photosynthesis: The natural process plants use to turn sunlight into food.

Temperate: Not too hot and not too cold – a moderate climate.

Torpor: A type of hibernation where an animal reduces its body temperature and metabolism.

Scavenge: To search for already-dead prey to eat.

Strand: When a marine mammal, like a whale or dolphin, accidentally becomes stuck on land.

CREDITS

First published in 2022
Australian Geographic
52-54 Turner Street
Redfern NSW 2016
02 9136 7206

editorial@ausgeo.com.au
australiangeographic.com.au

Photographs: Alamy; Australian Geographic; The Australian Museum; Getty; Shutterstock.

Printed by:
Leo Paper

Author: Karen McGhee
Editor: Martine Allars
Chief Sub-Editor: Serene Conneeley
Sub-Editor: Rachelle Mackintosh

Creative Director: Mike Ellott
Managing Picture Editor: Nicky Catley
Senior Designer: Mike Rossi

Print Production: Andy Franks
Commercial and Rights Manager:
Simone Aquilina

Australian Geographic
Managing Director: Jo Runciman